13142 362.299

www.heinemann.co.uk/library
Visit our website to find out more information about Heinemann Library books.

To order:
☎ Phone 44 (0) 1865 888066
📄 Send a fax to 44 (0) 1865 314091
💻 Visit the Heinemann Bookshop at www.heinemann.co.uk/library to browse our catalogue and order online.

Produced for Heinemann Library by White-Thomson Publishing Ltd, Bridgewater Business Centre, 210 High Street, Lewes, East Sussex, BN7 2NH.

First published in Great Britain by Heinemann Library, Jordan Hill, Oxford OX2 8EJ, part of Harcourt Education.

Heinemann Library is a registered trademark of Harcourt Education Ltd.

Consultant: Jenny McWhirter, Head of Education and Prevention, DrugScope
Editorial: Clare Collinson
Design: Tim Mayer
Picture Research: Amy Sparks
Production: Duncan Gilbert

Originated by P.T. Repro Multi Warna
Printed and bound in China, by South China Printing Company.

The paper used to print this book comes from sustainable resources.

The case studies and quotations in this book are based on factual examples. However, in some cases, the names or other personal information have been changed to protect the privacy of the individual concerned.

10 digit ISBN 0 431 10775 0 (hardback)
13 digit ISBN 978 0 431 10775 2 (hardback)
10 09 08 07 06
10 9 8 7 6 5 4 3 2 1

10 digit ISBN 0 431 10787 4 (paperback)
13 digit ISBN 978 0 431 10787 5 (paperback)
11 10 09 08 07
10 9 8 7 6 5 4 3 2 1

British Library Cataloguing in Publication Data
Fitzhugh, Karla
   Crystal meth and other amphetamines. – (What's the deal?)
   1. Ice (Drug) – Juvenile literature 2. Amphetamines – Juvenile literature 3. Amphetamine abuse – Juvenile literature
   I. Title
   362.2.'99
A full catalogue record for this book is available from the British Library.

Acknowledgements
The publisher would like to thank the following for their kind permission to use their photographs:

Alamy 6 (Photofusion Picture Library), 8 (David Hoffman Photo Library), 16–17 (Stephen Shepherd), 18–19 (Mikael Karlsson), 28 (Janine Wiedel Photolibrary), 33 (Janine Wiedel Photolibrary), 31 (Janine Wiedel Photolibrary), 50 (Jackson Smith); Corbis 9 (Houston Scott), 12 (Howard Sochurek), 15 (Reuters), 25 (Randy Faris), 29 (Bojan Brecelj), 30 (Jutta Klee), 25 (Jim Arbogast), 38–39 (Reuters), 40 (Andrew Lichtenstein), 43 (ER Productions), 48 (Bob Daemmrich), 49 (Gideon Mendel); Corbis Sygma 4–5 (Cambell William); Getty 10 (Photographer's Choice), 11 (Stone), 13 (Stone), 14 (Taxi), 23 (The Image Bank), 26–27 (Taxi), 36 (Taxi), 37 (The Image Bank), 42 (The Image Bank), 44–45 (Stone), 46–47 (The Image Bank), 51 (The Image Bank); Science Photo Library 6 (Cordelia Molloy); Topfoto 21 (Imageworks).

Cover artwork by Phil Weyman, Kralinator Design.

Every effort has been made to contact copyright holders of any material reproduced in this book. Any omissions will be rectified in subsequent printings if notice is given to the publishers.

Contents

❚ Words appearing in the text in bold, **like this**, are explained in the Glossary.

Crystal meth and other amphetamines – what's the deal?

Sixteen-year-old Katy used to hang out with some of her friends after school. Most of the time they would just watch TV, talk, or listen to music. The older boys in the group would sometimes smoke cigarettes or steal alcohol from their friends' parents. Katy had heard rumours that some of them had started smoking crystal meth. One evening, two of her friends smoked some of the drug in front of her. They offered Katy some.

"Seeing my friends using meth was just too scary. I don't see the appeal of staying up all night taking drugs. I've heard a lot of bad things about meth, like it's easy to get hooked, and it's made out of poisonous chemicals. I thought they were being so stupid. I don't ever want to try this stuff. It was easy to say no."

What would you have done if you were Katy? Do you know how you would cope with this difficult situation?

Crystal meth and other amphetamines are drugs that speed up some of the actions of the brain and body, making people feel temporarily alert and energetic. **Abusing** these drugs is very risky – it can make people seriously ill, damage their brain, and even kill them. It can

wreck personal relationships and land people with a conviction that could ruin a future career. These drugs are also **addictive** – some people find it very hard to stop taking them and the drugs completely take over their lives.

Making decisions

You might think that crystal meth and other amphetamines will never be an issue for you. But if you were offered one of these drugs by someone you know, what would you do? This book will give you the information you need to make up your own mind about the risks of crystal meth and other amphetamines. It looks at who abuses these drugs, and why they may be tempted to take them. It also looks at the harm these drugs can do to a user's health, and the other ways in which they can ruin a person's life.

▌Although it may look fairly harmless, crystal meth and other amphetamines have the power to wreck lives.

There are many issues to think about. Are the penalties for abusing these drugs strict enough? What is being done to tackle the problem of amphetamine abuse? Finally, what can be done to help addicts kick their habit? Let's take a hard look at crystal meth and other amphetamines.

What are crystal meth and other amphetamines?

Crystal meth and other amphetamines are all **synthetic** drugs that belong to a group of chemicals known as **stimulants**. Amphetamines were originally made as medicines, but nowadays they are used to treat only a few illnesses. Crystal meth is a street name for a certain type of amphetamine. Its effects are stronger than those of other amphetamines, and they last longer. All amphetamines have serious health risks, but many experts believe crystal meth can be even more harmful to a person's health than other amphetamines.

What are stimulants?

Stimulants are drugs that work by speeding up the activity in a person's brain, which affects their feelings and thoughts, and processes in the rest of the body. There are many different types of stimulant drugs. Some, such as caffeine (found in coffee, tea, and some soft drinks), have mild effects. Others, such as amphetamines, MDMA (ecstasy), and cocaine, have much stronger effects. In this book we shall be looking at amphetamines.

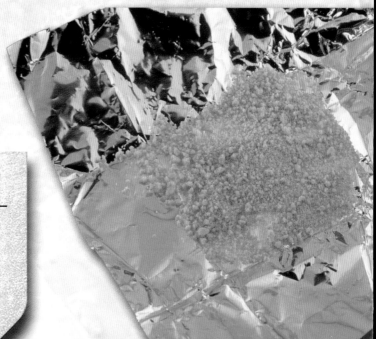

▌ Amphetamine powder may look off-white, greyish, or pinkish, depending on what chemicals have been used to make it.

⚠ Street names for amphetamines

Street names for amphetamines include: speed, phets, uppers, whizz, pep pills, P, and goey.

Amphetamine history

The first amphetamine was made in 1887 by a chemist in Germany. At first, little was known about this new chemical. It was not until 1927 that doctors discovered it had an effect upon the lungs and nasal · passages, and on the mind. From the 1930s onwards, amphetamines were **prescribed** for all kinds of health problems, such as asthma, low **blood pressure**, and mild depression. They were available to buy in shops without a **prescription** and some people took them for non-medical reasons. By the 1960s, doctors had realized that these drugs were **addictive** and had dangerous **side effects**, so they stopped prescribing them for most illnesses. Laws were brought in to make the sale of amphetamines illegal, unless a person had a prescription.

Amphetamines today

Nowadays, the medical use of amphetamines is very limited (see pages 10–11). Some people use amphetamines for non-medical reasons (sometimes called amphetamine **abuse**), which can be very risky to their health. These drugs may be medical drugs that have been stolen from pharmacies, hospitals, or factories, or obtained using a false prescription. But many of the amphetamines that are abused today are illegally made "street" amphetamines.

Forms of amphetamine

Amphetamines come in tablet form or as a powder. The tablets are usually swallowed, or crushed and **snorted** (sniffed up through the nose). Illegally made street amphetamines usually come in the form of a powder, tiny crystals, or a putty-like substance called "base". These forms of amphetamine are usually snorted, but sometimes they are swallowed, dabbed on to the gums, or prepared for injection.

I "Rocks" of crystal meth tend to look like ice crystals or crushed glass.

What is crystal meth?

Crystal meth is a form of **methamphetamine**, which is a type of amphetamine. Methamphetamine may appear in tablet form, as a fine powder, or as large crystals. It is the crystals that are known as crystal meth or "ice". The clear, colourless, or yellowish crystals look like crushed ice or broken glass.

Medical methamphetamine

The first methamphetamine was made by a Japanese chemist in 1919. It was tried as a treatment for many illnesses including depression, but was found to cause more health problems than it solved. It is still a **prescription** medicine in some countries but like other amphetamines, doctors rarely use it any more because it is **addictive** and has harmful **side effects**.

Methamphetamine abuse

It is thought that illegally-made crystal meth was first produced in South Korea and Taiwan, and introduced into the United States by drug gangs during the 1980s. Crystal meth **abuse** became more widespread in the 1990s and it is now one of the most commonly abused drugs in Thailand, Korea, and Japan. Its use has spread to Australia and all parts of the United States, and there is a high rate of abuse in Hawaii. Abuse of crystal meth is much less common in the United Kingdom than in the United States and Australasia. Almost all of the methamphetamine abused today is made in illegal secret laboratories using highly dangerous substances.

How is crystal meth different from other amphetamines?

Amphetamines all have major health risks, but many doctors believe that crystal meth is the most dangerous type of all. People have died after taking only a small amount of it. Crystal meth is also thought to be more addictive than other amphetamines, and it may lead to more aggressive and violent behaviour in users.

The effects of crystal meth are also stronger and longer lasting than the effects of other amphetamines. The drug is usually smoked or injected rather than swallowed or **snorted**. When taken in these ways, the drug affects the brain much more quickly than when it is snorted or swallowed. Abuse of methamphetamine has a serious effect on the user's brain chemistry, and many experts believe it may cause long-lasting brain damage.

❚ Some people who abuse crystal meth smoke the drug. They heat it up inside glass or metal pipes and inhale the fumes.

Medical use of amphetamines

There are very few uses for amphetamines in modern medicine. They are mainly used to treat two conditions: narcolepsy and ADHD (attention deficit hyperactivity disorder). Doctors have to keep a close eye on their patients to make sure they are giving them the right dose, and to make sure that the **side effects** do not outweigh the benefits of the medication.

What is narcolepsy?

Narcolepsy is a rare sleep problem, affecting about 2 in 10,000 people. People with narcolepsy may suddenly fall asleep during the day, and are completely unable to control this. The problem can make driving or cycling dangerous, and can affect schooling and employment. People with narcolepsy are often more able to stay awake during the day if they are **prescribed** small amounts of the amphetamine Dexedrine (dexamphetamine sulphate) or the amphetamine-like drug Ritalin (methylphenidate hydrochloride).

❚ Small doses of amphetamines can help people suffering from narcolepsy to stay awake during the day.

Question

Why are amphetamine-like drugs given to children with ADHD?

Attention deficit hyperactivity disorder (ADHD)

ADHD is the name given to a condition that involves a range of behaviour problems. People suffering from ADHD find it difficult to concentrate or pay attention to things. There are many ways in which children and adults with ADHD can be helped, and this may include giving them drugs. Ritalin is sometimes used to treat children with ADHD. It is not strictly an amphetamine, but it does have a very similar chemical structure. Nowadays, many doctors prefer not to prescribe Ritalin to teenagers and adults, owing to the risk of side effects and **addiction**.

❚ Children with ADHD often find it hard to concentrate, and may be disruptive at school. The amphetamine-like drug Ritalin seems to have a calming effect on children with this condition.

How safe are amphetamines from the doctor?

When doctors give amphetamines to a patient, they prescribe the smallest amount of the drug possible. They also monitor their patients to make sure the drugs are working, and that the patient feels well. If a patient takes the amphetamines exactly as the doctor has told them to, they are unlikely to suffer any bad effects. Doctors need to be aware of patients who might be taking too much of their medication, or doing something illegal, such as selling it.

Answer

Although amphetamine-like drugs tend to make adults feel more alert and awake, they often have a calming effect on children with ADHD who are **hyperactive**. The exact way that this works is not fully understood.

11

How do amphetamines work?

Amphetamines are drugs that stimulate the activity of the body's **central nervous system**. They increase the amounts of certain chemicals in the brain, making users feel temporarily wide awake and alert. They also bring about changes in the rest of the body. Most of these changes are unpleasant, or may have harmful effects on a person's health.

Question

Do amphetamines really give people more energy?

Changes in the brain

When amphetamines are taken, they are carried in the bloodstream to the nerve cells of the brain. Amphetamines make these cells release large amounts of certain chemicals in the brain, including the chemical **dopamine**. These chemicals have a strong effect on the rest of the brain, and on some of the nerves in the rest of

▌Amphetamines start to work when they get inside the cells of the brain, increasing the cells' activity.

the body. This brings about an increased sense of energy and alertness, and feelings of hunger are reduced. Users may feel more able to concentrate on certain tasks, although this does not necessarily mean that they can perform the tasks better.

Some of the effects of amphetamines on the brain and the changes they bring about make them useful as medicines for treating narcolepsy and ADHD (see pages 10–11). Other effects can be very harmful and long-term **abuse** of amphetamines can lead to brain damage (see pages 36–37).

The comedown

By the time the effects of amphetamines wear off, the amount of dopamine and other chemicals in some parts of the brain has dropped to a very low level. This is because they have been used up quickly, and the body takes time to replace them. This leaves the user feeling very tired and it can be a couple of days before they feel normal again. You can read more about these effects, sometimes called a **comedown**, on pages 24–25.

Changes in the body

Most of the body's actions are controlled by different areas of the brain. When someone takes amphetamines it changes the chemistry of their brain, causing a number of changes in the body. You can read more about these effects on page 22 of this book.

▌After the effects of amphetamines wear off, a person's brain takes a long time to recover.

Answer

No. These drugs trick the brain and body into thinking they have lots of energy. They make a person use up their energy reserves, necessary for the healthy function of their organs. Once the effects of the drugs wear off, the person is left feeling exhausted.

Why do people abuse amphetamines?

In spite of the serious health risks, a few people are tempted to take amphetamines for non-medical reasons. So what is it that drives some people to **abuse** these drugs?

Influences and pressures

There are many influences and pressures that can lead someone to start abusing crystal meth and other amphetamines. Sometimes, people are tempted to try them out of curiosity. They may also be feeling under pressure to fit in with a group. Although young people like to express their individual personalities, they also like to feel that they fit in with their friends. Other people may try amphetamines as part of a more general pattern of risk-taking. This could also include under-age smoking, taking a mixture of other illegal drugs, or drinking large amounts of alcohol.

Some people may be tempted to turn to amphetamines because they think the drugs will help them escape from their problems. However, after the effects of the drugs have worn off, the problems will still be there. Using drugs only makes a person's problems worse.

Dealer pressure

Some drug **dealers** work hard to sell drugs such as crystal meth and other amphetamines to young people. They know that once someone has tried these drugs there's a good chance that they will become **addicted**. This will provide the dealers with a regular source of income.

I The majority of young people never try crystal meth or other amphetamines.

The effects of the drugs

Some people abuse amphetamines because they think these drugs will help them to stay awake and alert when they are tired. These include some long-distance lorry drivers, people working night shifts, people who go to all-night nightclubs, and a few students who are preparing for exams. Of course, it is very dangerous to drive or operate machinery under the influence of drugs. Also, amphetamines do not remove the body's need for natural sleep. Lack of sleep can be very harmful to a person's health (see pages 32–33).

Many sportspeople are under pressure to improve their performance. A few of these people may give in to this pressure by taking drugs such as amphetamines. Most people agree that this is cheating. If someone is caught cheating in a competition they may be punished or lose their place in a team.

! Risks to students

Some students might be tempted to take amphetamines because they want to sit up all night studying for exams, but this is not a good idea. The drugs are bad for short-term memory, they can make exam stress feel much worse, and a student may end up so tired that they can't stay awake for the exam they have been studying for.

▌ Some sportspeople, including cyclists, are tempted to take amphetamines to overcome feelings of tiredness. This is cheating, and has led to deaths.

Amphetamine abuse today

The vast majority of teenagers never try crystal meth or other amphetamines. Those who do try them do not usually become regular users. However, many people who go through a period of regular amphetamine use find they become **addicted**.

First contact with amphetamines

The first contact most people have with crystal meth or other amphetamines is when they are offered them by a friend, or someone else they know. They are often offered them for free, although sometimes the friend may be trying to sell the drugs. This may happen at school or work, or at a party or nightclub. These drugs may also be offered to sportspeople who are training for competitions. Sometimes people are approached by drug **dealers** on the streets. Most people say no if they are offered these drugs. For more advice about how to deal with these situations, see pages 50–51.

Patterns of use

Some people try amphetamines once or twice, then decide that they don't like the effects, or the way they feel after the drugs have worn off. Other people use amphetamines occasionally, often at late-night parties or nightclubs. After a few months, they tend to stop taking them altogether. Only a few people go on to take these drugs on a regular basis, or over a period of years. Heavy users of amphetamines, especially people who regularly take crystal meth, may find that they have great difficulty giving the drugs up.

What are the statistics?

People in their late teens and early 20s are the age group most likely to try crystal meth and other amphetamines. In 2003 it was estimated that around two-thirds of the world's 33 million amphetamine users lived in Asia. The country with the highest levels of amphetamine **abuse** is Thailand, where between 5 and 7 per cent of the general population use amphetamines illegally.

During 2001, only about 1.1 per cent of all people in the United States aged 15 and over had taken amphetamines once or more. In the United Kingdom, amphetamine abuse seems to be decreasing. Around 3 per cent of people aged 16–59 tried amphetamines at least once in 1998, but this fell to 1.6 per cent in 2002, according to one recent UK study. Abuse of crystal meth is much less common in the United Kingdom than in the United States and Australasia. In Australia and New Zealand, use of amphetamines, especially crystal meth, has increased among young people in the last five years.

❚ Crystal meth and other amphetamines have been linked to the late-night club scene, in which people dance all night.

Illegal production

Some illegally sold amphetamines are medical drugs that have been stolen, but most have been made illegally in secret laboratories. Making amphetamines is a very dangerous process, with great risks to personal safety. If someone is caught making amphetamines illegally they are likely to face a long prison sentence.

Illegal laboratories

From the 1960s onwards, many people were **abusing** amphetamines that had been produced for medical use. To deal with this growing problem, governments passed laws to make sure that these drugs could only be given to patients with the permission of a doctor. This made the medical drugs harder to obtain. As demand for amphetamines was still increasing, people began to make their

Meth labs in the United States

During the 1990s, around 80 per cent of all the illegal drug laboratories discovered by the police in the United States were found to be making **methamphetamine**.

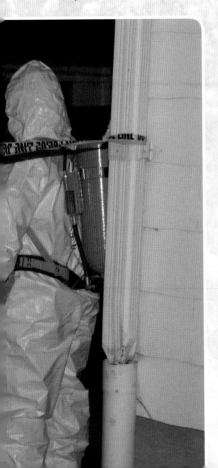

When officers investigate illegal laboratories where amphetamines are made, they have to wear protective clothing. The "labs" contain hazardous substances that may cause headaches, **nausea**, breathing problems, and eye irritations.

own versions of the drugs in illegal laboratories. Most amphetamines bought on the street are now made in this way by members of criminal gangs in the United States, Mexico, Australia, and Thailand.

Illegal laboratories may be very small, set up in suburban homes or hotel rooms, or they may be much larger. These laboratories are nothing like the laboratories where drugs are made legally. The people making amphetamines illegally are not scientists in clean white coats using advanced equipment. They do not follow health and safety rules, and the drugs are made in dirty, unhygienic conditions.

It is hard for police to find illegal laboratories making amphetamines, because they are often small and set up in secret locations, and they may be easily dismantled and moved.

"Cooking" with chemicals

When people make amphetamines illegally, they sometimes call the process "cooking" or "cooking up". Making crystal meth and other amphetamines can be very dangerous. The process involves the use of extremely hazardous substances, including battery acid, drain cleaner, and other poisonous chemicals. If spilled, they can cause deep chemical burns on the body. The cooking process also produces poisonous fumes and vapours, which are harmful to the environment. It also results in large quantities of **toxic** waste, which is often not disposed of safely. The ingredients may catch fire very easily, and explosions are also possible.

Are street drugs like medical drugs?

When crystal meth and other amphetamines are made illegally, many dangerous substances are involved in the process. There are no controls over the strength of the drugs and it is impossible for users to tell how pure or impure the drugs are. Other ingredients are often added to amphetamines so that **dealers** can make a bigger profit. Some of these substances can have unpleasant effects and be very harmful to a person's health.

⚠ The dealer's mix

Dealers mix amphetamines with a range of inexpensive products to make more money. These ingredients may include talcum powder, milk powder, glucose, laxatives, rock salt or other salt, chalk, cleaning products, vitamin C powder, aspirin, caffeine, and paracetamol. All these ingredients can be deadly if they are injected into the bloodstream, as they clot easily in the blood.

Dangers of pure and impure drugs

Making crystal meth and other amphetamines illegally isn't an exact process. Sometimes amphetamines are 99 per cent pure, but sometimes they may be as little as 2 per cent pure. This means that users cannot know how pure or strong illegally-made drugs are. Someone may accidentally take an **overdose** (too much of the drug) if the drugs turn out to be purer and stronger than they expected.

About drug dealers

Dealers often mix other less expensive ingredients with amphetamines to make them more bulky. This way they can make a bigger profit. They do not worry about the safety of the ingredients, as making money is their top priority. Many drug dealers also give out bad advice about drug safety. They may pretend to be someone's friend to gain their trust. Again, this is to help them sell drugs and make more money.

Other ingredients

Just about any cheap powder, granules, or paste may be mixed with street amphetamines. Dealers will use anything that's close to hand, cheap, or convenient. Sometimes drugs such as aspirin and paracetamol are ground up and added to the mixture. These drugs are bad for the liver and kidneys in large amounts, and it is possible to overdose on paracetemol and aspirin without even knowing you have taken them. Many other substances that would be more at home under a kitchen sink than inside a human body may be added to amphetamines.

▌Crystal meth and other amphetamines are made from a variety of chemicals and household products, many of which are poisonous.

The effects of amphetamines

Using crystal meth and other amphetamines affects individual people differently. When the actions of the drugs wear off there is an unpleasant "**comedown**". Even first-time users can suffer harmful effects.

Effects on the body

Once taken, it is usually a few minutes before amphetamines have a noticeable effect. The first effects of amphetamines on the body vary from person to person, but commonly:

- the heart starts to beat at a faster rate

- the rate of breathing increases

- the **blood pressure** starts to increase

- the mouth starts to feel dry

- sweating increases and the skin may be pale or flushed

- the pupils dilate or widen

- the temperature of the body increases

- **blood sugar levels** are raised

- the appetite is suppressed

- there is increased physical activity in adults

- coordination of movement is reduced, which may lead to shakiness or tremors.

Users may also have stomach cramps, vomiting, or diarrhoea. Some users complain of headaches, itchy skin, dizziness, or blurry vision.

As with all drugs, the way in which amphetamines are taken will make a difference to how quickly and how strongly

Question

How long do the effects of amphetamines last?

a person feels the effects. If amphetamines are swallowed, the effects come on more slowly than if they are injected.

When users smoke or inject crystal meth, its effects come on much faster and more strongly, as an almost-immediate "rush" or "hit".

Risks to health

The **abuse** of amphetamines can lead to serious physical harm, especially if the drugs are taken in large amounts. For example, because amphetamines have a powerful effect on the heart, making it beat faster, it is very risky for someone with a heart problem to take these drugs. You can read more about the harm amphetamines can do to the body on pages 32–33 of this book.

▌Crystal meth and other amphetamines may sometimes cause blurred vision and dizziness.

Answer

The first effects of a normal dose of amphetamines last for about 4 to 8 hours, but the effects of crystal meth may last up to 24 hours.

23

Effects on behaviour

Someone who has taken crystal meth or other amphetamines may appear more alert or chatty than usual and they may feel as if they have more energy. Often their speech will speed up, and the things they say make little or no sense to others.

> "When I came down I couldn't sleep, even though I was tired. My heart was about ready to come out of my chest, even a full day after I tried the drug. This was the first time I did uppers and I'm just not used to it. It's too scary."
>
> Jake, aged sixteen

People who have taken amphetamines tend to be fidgety, or unable to sit still, or have an urge to move around much more than normal. Their movements may be slightly shaky or less smooth and their hands may shake when they are sitting or standing still. Some users find themselves making the same movements over and over again, such as having the impulse to clean things obsessively.

Amphetamines may also make someone become over-confident, aggressive, or irritable. The use of crystal meth is especially likely to lead to violent behaviour. You can read more about the long-term effects of amphetamine **abuse** on a person's behaviour and mind on pages 34–37.

What is a comedown?

As we have seen, taking amphetamines causes the rapid release of natural chemicals such as **dopamine** in the brain. It takes a long time for the body to replace these chemicals, and by the time the effects of the drug wear off, there are very low levels of the chemicals in some parts of the brain. This chemical imbalance leaves the user feeling exhausted, irritable, and miserable. They may also be feeling the after-effects of other

There is a strong link between amphetamine abuse and aggressive behaviour.

substances that were mixed into the drugs, or they may be physically exhausted from too much activity, or from lack of sleep. These effects can last for several days. Sometimes, users are so tired that they sleep for up to 48 hours. A **comedown** from crystal meth may be much worse than one from other amphetamines, because meth has the strongest effects on the brain.

! The extra dangers of mixing drugs

Taking two drugs together can have a more powerful effect on the body than taking one drug alone. For example, taking amphetamines with other **stimulant** drugs can speed up the heart so much that it can't beat properly – this can cause death.

25

Risk of death

Amphetamines are drugs that make the heart beat faster. Most users find that their heartbeat feels irregular or that it is beating harder than usual. If blood is pumping around someone's body with increased force, there is a higher risk of the person suffering a **stroke**, in which the blood supply to part of the brain is cut off. Large amounts of crystal meth and amphetamines can make the heart beat so fast that it is unable to pump blood around the body properly. This can cause brain damage or death.

Crystal meth and other amphetamines can cause overheating, especially if the user is dancing somewhere warm for a long time. Overheating can make someone collapse from **heat stroke**. It can also lead to internal bleeding and death.

It is possible to take an **overdose** of crystal meth or other amphetamines. If a person takes too much of a drug, their body is unable to break it down, and they can become seriously ill or die. Signs of an overdose include confusion, **hallucinations** (seeing or hearing things that aren't really there), chest pain, difficulty in breathing, aggression, chills and fever, muscle spasms, **nausea**, and vomiting. In the most extreme cases people may have **seizures** (fits), or collapse and become unconscious.

❗ Methamphetamine emergencies

According to the US Drug Abuse Warning Network (DAWN), **methamphetamine**-related emergency room visits in the United States increased by over 30 per cent between 2000 and 2002, from 13,500 to 17,700.

I If someone becomes ill or collapses as a result of taking crystal meth or other amphetamines, it's important to call an ambulance right away.

What to do in an emergency

If you think someone has collapsed under the influence of drugs, or may have taken an overdose, you should call for an ambulance right away. If you know what drug the person has taken, tell the ambulance team – this could save the person's life and you won't get them into trouble. Do not offer coffee, alcohol, or other drinks to someone who has taken amphetamines as these can react with the drugs or be a choking hazard. Do not shout or scream at the person, as this can put more strain on the heart. If possible, talk to the person in a calm voice, get them to sit down or lie on their side, and stay with them until help arrives.

The dangers of injecting amphetamines

Some users of crystal meth and other amphetamines take the drugs by injecting them into their body with a needle. This is one of the most risky ways to take any drug. It seriously increases the chances of taking an **overdose**, damages the veins, and can lead to life-threatening infections.

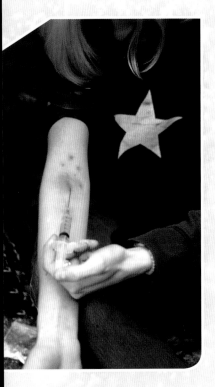

I Injecting drugs causes damage to the veins and harms other tissues all around the body.

Pure or impure?

As we have seen, it's impossible to tell what's in a dose of crystal meth or other amphetamines just by looking at it. Street amphetamines may be over 97 per cent impure. People may end up injecting talcum powder, milk powder, chalk, or **toxic** chemicals straight into their veins, which can make them seriously ill. Sometimes the drugs are purer than expected, so people may inject a much larger amount than they intended, all in one go. This can lead to an accidental overdose.

How do needles damage the body?

People who regularly inject drugs into their veins often find that their veins eventually close up, because of the damage this causes. The action of injecting can also put bubbles of air or lumps of drugs into the bloodstream, which may cut off the blood supply to the body's tissues. This may cause permanent damage to the tissues, and if it affects organs such as the heart or brain it can cause death or disability.

Injecting drugs into the veins often leads to scarring. Using dirty needles can also cause skin infections, including open, weeping sores and abscesses (a kind of large boil). Dirty needles can also result in

Dave's story

Dave is 27 years old and was addicted to amphetamines for eight years. He regularly injected the drugs into his body, but finally gave up using amphetamines when he realized he might need to have a leg amputated.

"I was told several times by doctors that if I carried on injecting, I would lose a leg. That really scared me because I know some people who have lost a leg or an arm or fingers or toes. I've got messed-up legs. I've got holes in my body. I have hepatitis C and plenty of scars. I think I'm actually very lucky to be alive."

blood poisoning. In some cases, users suffering from blood poisoning have to have a limb amputated.

What about shared needles?

People who inject drugs often do not have access to clean needles and syringes, which increases the risks of infection. Many users end up sharing needles with other people. This means that any infections they have are easily passed on. Some of these infections are life-threatening, including **HIV** (the virus that causes AIDS) and **hepatitis B** and **C** (which can seriously damage the liver).

▌When people inject crystal meth or other amphetamines, they often do this in unhygienic conditions and with dirty needles. This leads to the spread of infections.

Amphetamines and addiction

Many people who take crystal meth or other amphetamines for a period of time find it very difficult to stop using the drugs. The need for drugs can take over a person's life, and be very difficult to break free from. People can come to depend on all forms of amphetamine, but crystal meth is thought to be especially **addictive**.

How does addiction start?

When someone takes amphetamines regularly, they usually find that they need to take larger and larger doses of the drugs to get the same effect. This is called developing a **tolerance** to the drugs. Addiction can develop as a person comes to depend upon the effects of amphetamines. They may start to use the drugs just to avoid the bad feelings that happen when the drugs start to wear off. These include unbearable **cravings**, and **withdrawal symptoms** such as feelings of depression and tiredness.

▌When people become addicted, they may be so desperate for money to buy more amphetamines that they turn to crime.

Many regular users of amphetamines develop a **psychological dependence** on the drugs. This means they feel unable to cope with everyday life without a supply of the drug.

How quickly can someone become addicted?

It's often impossible to tell who will become addicted to amphetamines and who won't. Many amphetamine addicts say that their addiction crept up on them unexpectedly. Others say that after the first time they tried crystal meth they felt as if they had to take more. Many regular users only realize they have a problem when their supply of drugs runs out. When someone is addicted, the drugs take over their life, and may become more important than family, friends, children, schooling or work, or any interests.

! Signs of addiction

Early signs of addiction may include a person:

- spending most of the day thinking about, trying to find, or using the drugs

- feeling that they need amphetamines just to get through the day

- becoming secretive or lying about their behaviour

- becoming anxious if they can't get hold of the drugs

- spending less time on their usual activities and interests

- stealing from family or friends to get money for drugs.

Leonie's story

Once someone becomes hooked on amphetamines, they may begin to lie and steal to fund their habit. When Leonie's nineteen-year-old son stole from her to get money to buy amphetamines, she decided that drastic action was necessary.

"I am feeling just about as low as you can get. He is my son. And I had him arrested. He has stolen from me – at home, at work, and even while I was in the hospital. He basically cleaned me out. TVs, DVD players, movies, and music, he even took my books right off the shelves."

The risks of long-term abuse

Long-term use of crystal meth and other amphetamines causes the body to become very run down. It weakens a person's **immune system** and causes permanent damage to many different parts of the body.

Wear and tear on the body and teeth

Because they make people feel temporarily more energetic, amphetamines tend to make people push their bodies much further than they should do. They may keep going for long periods when their bodies are desperate for rest. This causes physical wear and tear on their body, including muscles, bones, and joints.

Amphetamines can cause tension in the muscles and a tightness of the jaw that leads some people to grind their teeth and chew constantly. In the long term this grinding can wear the teeth down and, in some cases, **addicts** may crush their teeth to powder through continual grinding.

! Weak bones and bad teeth

Many amphetamine users have poor diets, lacking in healthy minerals such as calcium that are needed for strong bones. The drug also reduces the body's ability to absorb calcium. Add in extra wear and tear from too much physical activity, and teeth-grinding caused by the drugs, and you have a recipe for weak bones and bad teeth.

Why do users get so run down?

Amphetamines may make people feel as if they don't need to sleep, but these drugs do not remove a person's need for sleep. Natural sleep is vital to a person's physical and mental health.

Amphetamines may make users feel as if they are not hungry, but they do not provide energy or remove the body's need for food. A healthy diet is a basic human need, but amphetamine users often skip meals or eat junk food. This leads to a lack of essential vitamins, minerals, and energy, and wasting of the body.

This lack of sleep and good food can weaken the immune system, the body's defence against bacteria and viruses. Users find that they catch colds and flu more often, and their skin is more likely to break out in acne spots or sores.

What about the body's organs?

Long-term **abuse** of amphetamines affects the whole body. It can lead to stomach ulcers and bleeding, and problems with the bowels. It can cause raised **blood pressure**, heart disease, an enlarged heart, and an increased risk of heart attacks. It has also been shown to cause liver damage. Vapours from smoking crystal meth damage the lungs and nasal passages. There is strong evidence that it can permanently damage the brain. You can read more about the risks to the brain and mental health on pages 34–37.

▋ Crystal meth and other amphetamines mess up a person's natural sleep pattern, and soon users become tired, unhealthy, and washed out.

The risks to mental health

A single dose of amphetamines can seriously affect someone's brain chemistry, and long-term **abuse** may damage the brain. This affects physical functions such as movement and speech. Amphetamines also affect the user's mental health, causing problems with moods and behaviour.

Amphetamines and anxiety

Amphetamines or crystal meth often make people feel frightened, anxious, tense, or stressed out. People who take amphetamines might also have **panic attacks** (sudden feelings of complete panic, as if something terrible is about to happen). They may feel as if they're about to die, or that they're in terrible danger.

Amphetamines and paranoia

People who take amphetamines and crystal meth often feel bad-tempered or suspicious of the people around them. At higher doses, they may imagine that someone or something is out to get them or wants to hurt or harm them in some way. This is called **paranoia**. They may take strange or dangerous action to defend themselves from the person they wrongly think is about to attack them. If someone is strongly paranoid, there is

> "My friend Karl got some meth and by the end of the next day he was so paranoid. He was completely afraid that there was a 'kid' waiting outside his apartment window to steal stuff, to break it, to do whatever. We went to his place to 'rescue' him and he was standing in the middle of his living room, holding a hammer, staring out the window. This is a nice, friendly guy we're talking about. And meth totally made him lose his mind."
>
> Sarah, aged twenty

no way to reason with them about their mistaken thinking. If someone with existing mental health problems abuses amphetamines, it can make the problems much, much worse.

Amphetamine psychosis

A single large dose of crystal meth or other amphetamines can bring on a condition called **amphetamine psychosis**. When a person is suffering from this condition, they may have **hallucinations**, in which they see or hear things that aren't really there. They may also become deeply paranoid and have strange ideas or behaviour. They will probably not think they have anything wrong with them. In many cases, people with this condition need expert medical care in hospital as they could become violent and be a danger to themselves or others. The effects of the drugs should wear off when all the amphetamines have been broken down by the body and passed out in the urine. This process may take a few days.

❙ Amphetamine abuse can cause mild or severe paranoia and other irrational thoughts.

Brain damage

There is good evidence to suggest that long-term **abuse** of crystal meth or other amphetamines can damage a person's brain. When amphetamines are abused over a long period, cells in important areas of the brain stop working properly, and connections between the cells become damaged.

This damage can have a wide range of effects, including changes in movement, thoughts, and moods. Some users find they have difficulty with their speech. Long-term use may also cause people to develop problems with their memory. They may have difficulty remembering recent events or things that happened a long time ago. They may also feel confused for a lot of the time, or behave or talk as though they are not able to think clearly. Some people develop odd little repetitive movements called "tics". They may develop strange habits that they carry out over and over again, in an obsessive way.

❚ Many amphetamine abusers say they feel depressed for long periods after they stop taking the drugs.

Other effects on the mind

There are many possible kinds of damage to the way the mind works. Heavy use of crystal meth or other amphetamines commonly leads to feelings of deep depression, when a person feels complete misery and unhappiness for long periods of time. They may be tempted to harm themselves. Sometimes users have rapid mood swings. They may lose touch with reality and become deluded. When someone is deluded they may wrongly feel they are a very powerful or famous person. They may have **hallucinations**. Amphetamines are also associated with violent and antisocial behaviour (see page 42). Many experts believe that users of crystal meth are most at risk of suffering these symptoms. This is because this drug is the strongest of all amphetamines.

"I'd rather eat rusty nails than take another hit of that stuff. Although rusty nails probably aren't that healthy, at least I know my brain is not going to fry any more. All that stuff does is make me lazy, unmotivated, undetermined, and depressed. What a pointless thing to do."

Tom, aged 22

Lack of sleep and mental health

As we have seen, amphetamine abuse messes up natural sleep patterns, making users feel very run down. If someone does not get enough sleep, they have difficulty concentrating, and can become moody and irrational.

▌Lack of natural sleep has harmful effects on a person's mental health.

Amphetamines and the law

Governments all around the world have passed laws to prevent the **abuse** of amphetamines. It is illegal for someone to use them without the permission of a doctor, or give them or sell them to someone else. A conviction for any drug offence can seriously affect a person's future, and many countries will refuse visas to people who have been convicted of a drug offence.

❗ Methamphetamine seizures

- Australian customs officers detected 324 kilograms (714 pounds) of methamphetamine during the year 2001 to 2002.

- In 2003, Taiwanese authorities seized 1,855 kilograms (4,090 pounds) of methamphetamine, 48 kilograms (106 pounds) of semi-finished methamphetamine, and 10 methamphetamine laboratories.

Classification of amphetamines

In the United Kingdom amphetamines are **prescription**-only Class B drugs. It is possible for doctors to **prescribe** them to patients, but it is illegal to be in **possession** of these drugs without a prescription. It is also an offence to **supply** them. If they are prepared for injection they become Class A drugs, along with drugs such as cocaine and heroin.

❘ Police forces around the world work hard to prevent drug trafficking. These bags of crystal meth are part of a large shipment seized by Chinese police.

In Australia, amphetamines are Schedule 2 drugs. In New Zealand, most amphetamines are Class B drugs, but **methamphetamine** was reclassified as a Class A drug in 2003.

Possession

Possession simply means that someone has control over an amount of a drug. They may be carrying a small amount of the drug on their body, for example in a pocket or a bag, or they may be keeping the drugs somewhere, such as in a school or gym locker or in a drawer in a bedroom. If someone is caught with a large amount of amphetamines, the police may assume that it is not for their own personal use, and may charge them with "possession with intent to supply".

▌Drug dealers face heavy fines and prison sentences if they are caught.

Supply

Supply means giving or selling the amphetamines to other people. People who sell drugs are usually called **dealers**. Simply giving a tiny amount of amphetamines to a friend for free can lead to someone being arrested for supplying drugs.

Other drug laws

Making amphetamines without official government permission is illegal. **Smuggling** amphetamines, or some of their ingredients, between different states or countries is called **trafficking**, and can lead to a long prison sentence.

█ In some countries, young drug users are sent to prison, and are not offered treatment for their **addiction**.

Punishing offenders

In the United Kingdom, where amphetamines are classified as Class B drugs, **possession** of these drugs can lead to up to five years in jail and a fine. **Supplying** someone else can bring a maximum of fourteen years in prison and an unlimited fine. If amphetamines are prepared for injection they become Class A drugs. If someone is caught with them in their possession they may face seven years in prison, and supplying amphetamines prepared for injection could lead to life imprisonment.

In Australia, where amphetamines are also classified as Class B drugs, penalties vary from state to state. For example, in the state of Victoria, possession can lead to a year in prison and a fine of up to Aus$3,000 (£1,200). Supply and **trafficking** have heavier sentences of up to 25 years in prison, a fine of Aus$250,000 (£100,000), or both.

In New Zealand, **methamphetamine** has recently been reclassified as a Class A drug, with higher penalties for use and supply. Being caught supplying methamphetamine in New Zealand could now lead to a life sentence in prison.

VIEWPOINTS

Some governments are considering harsher punishments for people who **abuse** amphetamines. Countries such as New Zealand have already increased the punishments for people who take crystal meth. Some people say that having harsher penalties is the best way to stop people abusing drugs, but others disagree.

- **The law should be tougher on users of amphetamines**
Crystal meth and other amphetamines are very dangerous drugs. Increasing the punishment for users of these drugs sends out a very strong message about the health risks. Users will be less likely to take or sell drugs if they face a large fine or a long prison sentence.

- **Punishing people more harshly is not the best approach**
Giving up amphetamines can be very hard, and users need treatment, not punishment. The money spent on keeping people in prison would be better spent on educating people about the dangers of drugs. Governments should target drug suppliers, not drug users.

What do you think?

Wider effects

Some people think that if someone chooses to use amphetamines, they aren't hurting anybody else but themselves. But taking amphetamines doesn't just affect the lives of the users. It causes problems and distress to many others, including family, friends, and children. It also causes many problems for our society – especially for those who have to deal with the damage it causes.

I Abuse of amphetamines has been linked to many incidents of domestic violence.

Victims of violence

Violent and aggressive behaviour is common among people who use amphetamines – especially those who use crystal meth. As a result, many people become the victims of violence, including friends and family.

Children at risk

The children of people who **abuse** crystal meth and other amphetamines face a range of hazards as they grow up with drugs as part of their everyday life. Parents who are under the influence of amphetamines for much of the time may not be able to look after their children properly. Children may be accidentally injured by needles and they may face the daily reality of seeing their parents injecting themselves with drugs.

Some children may be exposed to **toxic** chemicals because an illegal laboratory has been set up in their home. Exposure to the poisonous substances involved in the illegal manufacture of amphetamines can cause damage to the skin, eyes, lungs, liver, and brain, and if they get on to the skin they can cause serious burns. Some of the poisonous chemicals used in these laboratories can cause death if they are inhaled or swallowed.

Amphetamine abuse during pregnancy

If a woman abuses meth or other amphetamines during pregnancy, there is a risk that the foetus (unborn child) will be seriously harmed. The baby may be born **addicted** to the drugs, or have heart problems. Normal development might be slowed, and there could be damage to the brain.

❚ Babies born to amphetamine addicts may suffer from a range of health problems. If they are born addicted to the drugs, they may experience unpleasant **withdrawal symptoms**.

Viewpoints

Some states in the United States send pregnant drug users to jail to protect their unborn children. People have different veiws about this policy.

● **Sending pregnant drug users to jail protects unborn children**

The state has a duty to protect children from drugs. An unborn child has no choice about being exposed to drugs. Putting an addicted woman in jail is the best way to force her to stop taking drugs.

● **Prison is not the best way to help pregnant users**

Pregnant amphetamine users need education, help, and support, not punishment. Drug users can still get hold of drugs in prison, so putting people in jail won't protect unborn children. Being forced to give birth wearing a prison uniform or handcuffs is traumatic and degrading.

What do you think?

When people are arrested by the police, they are often under the influence of various drugs. Surveys have shown that:

- in Australia in 2001, between 9 per cent and 22 per cent of people who were arrested tested positive for amphetamines

- in England and Wales in 2001, 9 per cent of arrested people had recently taken amphetamines.

Harm to the environment

The production of crystal meth and other amphetamines in illegal laboratories has a serious impact on the environment. In particular, when **methamphetamine** is made, poisonous gases are released into the air and large amounts of **toxic** waste are created. The people who operate these labs don't worry about how they dispose of this waste – often they will just put it down household drains or even straight onto roads or fields.

Dealing with crime

When people are dependent on amphetamines they often become desperate, and may commit crimes such as burglaries or muggings to get more money for drugs. These crimes can be devastating for the people who are targeted. The police have a difficult job tracking down drug **smugglers**, **dealers**, and users, as well as investigating the violent crimes associated with amphetamine **abuse**.

Problems at work

When someone is using drugs they may not always do their job properly. This can lead to accidents at work, in which the drug user or other people may be injured. Drug users often need to take days off work because of health problems. This may make life difficult for the people who work with them, and can cost a business a lot of money. It may also lead to the drug user losing their job, which can cause money problems for their family.

❚ Dealing with the crimes associated with drug use takes up a lot of police time and money. Taking people to court and sending them to prison puts a strain on the legal system.

Medical care

When users **overdose** or have bad reactions to amphetamines they need emergency medical care and time in hospital. Long-term users often develop all sorts of health problems, and treatment is needed for these too. This takes up the time and resources of busy doctors, nurses, and ambulance staff.

*"The patients are **paranoid**, wild-eyed, out of control, and making no sense. The challenge is to protect the patient from injuring themselves ... They become incredibly strong. They bite, kick, and have no respect for anyone."*

Dr Allan Reishus, who works in a hospital emergency room in Colorado, United States, describing patients who have overdosed on crystal meth

Giving up amphetamines

How easy is it to stop using crystal meth and other amphetamines? For some people the process isn't at all easy. People who are **addicted** to amphetamines experience unpleasant **withdrawal symptoms** when they give up. Once they have stopped using the drugs, they then need to learn how to stay off the drugs and cope with life without them.

Detoxification

When someone who is addicted to amphetamines stops taking the drugs, they go through a process known as **detoxification** (or detox). During this process, the person's body adjusts to living without the drug inside it. The person is likely to suffer a range of unpleasant withdrawal symptoms. For up to three days, they will probably feel exhausted, sleepy, and miserable. After four to seven days they are likely to feel completely run down, and have feelings of deep depression, anxiety, hunger, and irritability. They may also feel **paranoid** or have **hallucinations**. After the first week, these symptoms begin to go away. However, the person may have trouble sleeping and have strong **cravings** for the drugs for some months after giving them up.

I In group therapy, drug users are able to talk about their experiences, and support one another. This helps many people to stay away from drug abuse for good.

Rehabilitation

If amphetamines have become central to a person's life, it can be hard to stay off the drugs and adjust to life without them. After a period of addiction, many people need help putting their lives back together. This includes mending relationships with family and friends, and getting back into education or work. This process is sometimes called **rehabilitation** or "rehab".

What help is available?

Some people who give up amphetamines go through the process of detoxification by staying as a patient in a hospital or drug treatment centre. Others give up at home with the help of a doctor. People who need support during the process of rehabilitation may find **counselling** or other forms of **therapy** very helpful. Counselling or therapy allows people to talk through their problems and find ways of coping without drugs. There are also many drug agencies that offer support and advice.

How can amphetamine abuse be prevented?

Preventing the **abuse** of drugs such as crystal meth and other amphetamines is a very complicated problem. Governments have passed laws that send out a clear message that amphetamine abuse is illegal, but what else is being done to prevent the abuse of amphetamines?

Reducing the supply and demand

Customs officers and special police squads work hard to reduce the supply of illegally sold drugs. Specially trained officers are employed to find and shut down the secret laboratories where crystal meth and other amphetamines are produced. Many countries have introduced tight border controls to try to prevent drug **smuggling**. Specially trained officers use scanning machines and sniffer dogs to root out hidden drugs. They also catch people who are illegally transporting certain ingredients to make the drugs. Drug squads are also trained to track down **dealers**.

To help cut down demand, government departments, health services, schools, and youth organizations provide information about drug issues, and get people talking and thinking about

❚ Police forces use many methods to catch drug smugglers, including specially trained sniffer dogs.

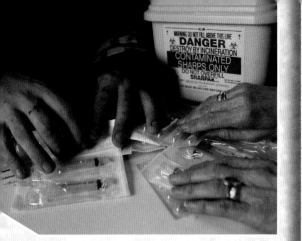

▌ Some health centres provide clean needles to amphetamine injectors. This has helped to prevent the spread of infections such as HIV.

the subject. Many schools have introduced programmes that teach young people about the risks of drug abuse. In this way, it is hoped that young people will feel able to make informed, healthy decisions.

Zero tolerance

Some schools operate a policy of "zero tolerance" towards pupils who use drugs. This means that any pupil who is caught using drugs or with drugs in their possession will be automatically punished. In some schools, a pupil is first given a warning, or they may be temporarily suspended. In other schools pupils may be expelled immediately. Some people believe that harsh action like this helps to prevent drug abuse. Others argue that a better approach is to offer **counselling** and education about drugs while allowing the students to remain in school.

Viewpoints

Should injecting users have access to clean needles? Health centres in some cities have "needle exchanges", where users are given clean needles. Some people think this helps to prevent some of the harm done by drug abuse. Others disagree.

- ### Needle exchanges prevent the spread of disease
  Studies have shown that needle exchange programmes help to prevent the spread of infections such as **HIV** among drug users. They are also good places to give out health information and offer counselling to give up drugs.

- ### Needle exchanges send out the wrong message
  Needle exchanges allow injectors to keep on using drugs. Using crystal meth and other amphetamines is illegal, and needle exchanges encourage people to keep using them.

What do you think?

Help and advice

Do you want to know more about crystal meth and other amphetamines, or are you worried about somebody who might be using drugs? There are many people and organizations you can contact for help and advice.

Finding out more

If you'd like to read more about crystal meth and other amphetamines, many schools, colleges, and libraries have leaflets or books that you can take away or borrow. There are also many organizations that provide reliable information about drugs. Some of these organizations are listed on pages 54–55 of this book. Many of them have useful websites, and some supply information packs.

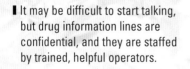

I It may be difficult to start talking, but drug information lines are confidential, and they are staffed by trained, helpful operators.

Someone to talk to

Sometimes it can be hard to talk to people you know about the things that are worrying you. If you want to ask questions **in confidence**, your school or college may have somebody to talk to, such as a school nurse or **counsellor**. Many organizations run telephone helplines staffed by specially trained advisers. Some of these helplines are open 24 hours a day, so you can call them for advice and information whenever you like. Remember, you don't have to have a drug problem yourself to call. You will find details of these helplines on pages 54–55 of this book.

Worried about someone else?

If you're worried about someone else's drug use, don't feel that you have to bottle all your feelings up and try to cope on your own. There are many organizations, groups, and charities you can contact for help and support. You could also talk to your local doctor or nurse, or call a helpline. You'll feel much better talking about your concerns.

It's your decision

One day someone might offer you drugs such as crystal meth or other amphetamines. It's important to think hard about how you would react. It helps to plan ahead, so that you can cope better with the situation. Here are some things to remember:

- be prepared – think over what you'll say in advance

- never forget the dangers – taking crystal meth or other amphetamines can really ruin your health and your life

- whatever people say, it's OK to say no to drugs

- you are not alone – there are many people your age in the same situation who don't use drugs

- it's your life – nobody else can tell you what to do and it's up to you to make your own decisions.

❚ Most teenagers make a healthy choice, and decide never to try drugs such as crystal meth or other amphetamines.

Glossary

abuse use of drugs for non-medical reasons in a way that has a bad effect

addiction when a person is unable to manage without a drug and finds it extremely hard to stop using it

amphetamine psychosis serious mental disorder in which a person loses touch with reality and experiences strong feelings of paranoia or hallucinations as a result of amphetamine abuse

blood pressure pressure of the blood as it circulates around the body

blood sugar level level of glucose (a type of sugar) in the blood

central nervous system network of nerves that runs from the brain through the spine and controls all the movements in the body

comedown feelings of tiredness experienced as the effects of a drug wear off, caused by a chemical imbalance in the brain

counselling advice and guidance given to people to help resolve their problems

counsellor person trained to give advice and guidance to people to help resolve their problems

craving strong or uncontrollable need or longing

dealer person who buys and sells drugs illegally

detoxification when all traces of a drug are gradually removed from a person's body

dopamine chemical in the brain that is associated with feelings of pleasure

hallucination experience of seeing or hearing something that is not really present and only exists in the mind

heat stroke medical condition caused by the failure of the body's natural temperature regulation system

hepatitis B and **C** diseases caused by a virus that can seriously damage the liver

HIV virus that can lead to AIDS

hyperactive extremely or abnormally active

immune system the body's natural defence against infection

in confidence privately, without telling anyone else

methamphetamine type of amphetamine that has strong effects

nausea feeling of wanting to vomit

overdose excessive dose of a drug which the body cannot cope with

panic attack sudden very strong feeling of anxiety, which makes a person's heart race

paranoia mental condition involving feelings of suspicion and distrust – a sense that everyone is out to get you, or to criticize your behaviour or actions

possession owning or having an illegal drug (either carrying it or having it hidden somewhere)

prescribe when a doctor or dentist writes an instruction (a prescription) that authorizes a medicine to be issued to a patient

prescription instruction written by a doctor or dentist which authorizes a pharmacist to issue a drug to a patient

psychological dependence when a person feels they need drugs to get through everyday life and cannot cope without them

rehabilitation process of returning to ordinary healthy life after a period of addiction

seizure sudden attack in which the body goes into spasm, seen in epilepsy or sometimes when a person takes an overdose of a drug

side effect unwanted effect of a drug or medical treatment

smuggle move goods illegally out of or into a country

snort take a drug by sniffing it up the nose

stimulant drug that speeds up the activity of the brain, making people feel alert and full of energy

stroke sudden change in the blood supply to part of the brain. A stroke can cause loss of physical functions such as movement or speech.

supply give or sell drugs to other people

synthetic made artificially using chemicals

therapy treatment that helps someone to get better. Therapy often involves talking to a counsellor.

tolerance need for larger and larger doses of a drug to get the same effect

toxic poisonous

trafficking smuggling or transporting drugs, usually in large amounts and across the borders of different countries

withdrawal symptoms unpleasant physical and mental feelings experienced during the process of giving up an addictive drug

Contacts and further information

There are a number of organizations that provide information and advice about drugs. Some have helpful websites, or provide information packs and leaflets, while others offer help and support over the phone.

Contacts in the UK

Adfam
Waterbridge House, 32–36 Loman Street, London SE1 0EH
Tel: 020 7928 8898
www.adfam.org.uk
Adfam is a national charity that gives confidential support and information to families and friends of drug users. They also run family support groups.

Childline
Tel: 0800 1111
A 24-hour number for any young person in distress to call. It offers confidential help and guidance from trained counsellors on a range of issues, including family problems caused by drugs.

Connexions Direct
Helpline: 080 800 13219 (8 a.m.–2 a.m. daily)
Text: 07766 4 13219
www.connexions-direct.com
This service for young people aged thirteen to nineteen offers information and advice on a wide range of topics, including drugs.

DrugScope
32–36 Loman Street, London SE1 0EE
Tel: 020 7928 1211
www.drugscope.org.uk
A national drugs information agency with services that include a library, a wide range of publications, and a website.

Families Anonymous
Doddington & Rollo Community Association, Charlotte Despard Avenue, Battersea, London SW11 5HD
Helpline: 0845 1200 660
www.famanon.org.uk
An organization involved in support groups for parents and families of drug users. They can put you in touch with groups in different parts of the country.

FRANK
Tel: 0800 776600
Email: frank@talktofrank.com
www.talktofrank.com
An organization for young people that gives free, confidential advice and information about drugs 24 hours a day.

Narcotics Anonymous
UK Service Office, 202 City Road, London EC1V 2PH
Helpline: 020 7730 0009 (10 a.m.– 10 p.m. daily)
www.ukna.org
A fellowship of people who have given up narcotics, using a twelve-step programme similar to the one used by Alcoholics Anonymous.

Release
Helpline: 0845 4500 215 (10 a.m.–5.30 p.m. Mon–Fri)
Email: ask@release.org.uk
www.release.org.uk
An organization that provides legal advice to drug users, their families, and friends. The advice is free, professional, non-judgemental, and confidential.

Contacts in Australia and New Zealand

Alcohol & Other Drugs Council of Australia (ADCA)
17 Napier Close, Deakin, ACT 2600
Tel: 02 6281 1002
www.adca.org.au
ADCA works to prevent or reduce the harm caused by drugs.

Australian Drug Foundation
409 King Street, West Melbourne, VIC 3003
Tel: 03 9278 8100
www.adf.org.au
An organization that works to prevent and reduce drug problems.

The DARE (Drug Abuse Resistance Education) Foundation of New Zealand
PO Box 50744, Porirua, New Zealand
Tel: 04 238 9550
www.dare.org.nz
An organization that provides drug prevention education programmes.

Foundation for Alcohol and Drug Education (FADE)
9 Anzac Street, PO Box 33–1505, Takapuna, Auckland, New Zealand
Tel: 09 489 1719
www.fade.org.nz
A national organization that provides services throughout the country.

Narcotics Anonymous
Australian Service Office, 1st Floor, 204 King Street, Newtown, NSW 2042
National helpline: 1300 652 820
http://na.org.au/
The Australian division of Narcotics Anonymous has helplines for users and their friends and relatives, plus events and meetings around Australia.

Turning Point
54–62 Gertrude Street, Fitzroy, VIC 3065
Helpline (DirectLine): 1800 888 236
www.turningpoint.org.au
Turning Point provides specialist treatment and support services to people affected by alcohol and drugs.

Further reading

Dr Miriam Stoppard's Drug Information File: From Alcohol and Tobacco to Ecstasy and Heroin, by Miriam Stoppard (Dorling Kindersley, 1999)

Drugs and You, by Bridget Lawless (Heinemann Library, 2000)

Drugs: The Truth, by Aidan Macfarlane and Ann McPherson (Oxford University Press, 2003)

Health Issues: Drugs, by Sarah Lennard-Brown (Hodder Children's Books, 2004)

Need to Know: Amphetamines, by Sean Connolly (Heinemann Library, 2000)

Teen Issues: Drugs, by Joanna Watson and Joanna Kedge (Raintree, 2004)

Why Do People Take Drugs?, by Patsy Westcott (Hodder Children's Books, 2000)

Wise Guides: Drugs, by Anita Naik (Hodder Children's Books, 1997)

Further research

If you want to find out more about problems related to crystal meth and other amphetamines, you can search the Internet, using a search engine such as Google. Try using keywords such as:

Crystal meth + addiction
Amphetamines + law
Methamphetamine + risks
Drugs + needle exchange
Drugs + zero tolerance

Index